A Pocket Book of Poems

to Accompany

the Life Launch Series

By: Dr. Liz Bataille

Publisher: LB Press Self-Publishing

Mind, Body, Spirit Healing

or disruption caused by errors or omissions, whether such errors or omissions result from negligence, accident, or any other cause.

Adherence to all applicable laws and regulations, including international, federal, state, and local governing professional licensing, business practices, advertising, and all other aspects of doing business in the US, Canada, or any other jurisdiction, is the sole responsibility of the reader and consumer. Neither the author nor the publisher assumes any responsibility or liability whatsoever on behalf of the consumer or reader of this material, and cannot be held responsible for the use of the information provided within. Any perceived slight of any individual or organization is purely unintentional.

<u>Dedication</u>

Dedicated to all writers - it is my wish that this work may inspire you to finish, start or find motivation to continue putting to paper your own stories. Also, dedicated to all teens and young adults - may this book help you to find your voice, to heal, or simply to process your experiences so that you may find more joy, peace, contentment and understanding in the world.

Dedicated to my son - it is my sincerest hope that you can see that I have done everything within my power and have worked very hard to provide for you a much improved, healthier experience of growing up in our home, compared to that which I experienced through my teen and young adult years.

I love you with all my heart, mind and soul, Boychick!

More by the Author

Dr. Liz Bataille: Amazon #1 Multi-International Best-Selling Author, Speaker, Founder: The BJD Rainbow of Hope Foundation for Suicide Prevention and Mental Health

Books/Publications

Life Launch! Surviving the Storms of Physical and Sexual Abuse, https://www.amazon.com/dp/B07V3N3YL5

PTSD Compass Book 1, Dr. Liz contributor, authors: Pantea Kalhor et al

https://amzn.to/3zBGRNw

Speak for Wealth Magazine, October 2021, pg 16

Tap-In Magazine, June 2022, Cover and pg. 8

Courses

Webinar: www.mbshealinginstitute/webinars

Social Media

Website: www.drlizlifelaunch.com (for FREEBIES! Incl free review copy of AUDIOBOOK, while supplies last)

LinkedIn: https://www.linkedin.com/in/dr-liz-lizette-bataille-phd-19a763198/

Amazon Author page: www.amazon.com/Dr-Liz-Bataille/e/B07V489XDM/

Facebook: www.facebook.com/lizette.bataille.3

FB business: https://www.facebook.com/drlizlifelaunch

YouTube

Channel: https://www.youtube.com/channel/UCJ1MOks73tYe y7tZMP84Eeg

Instagram: https://www.instagram.com/drlizlifelaunch/

Twitter:

http://twitter.com/DrLizMBSHealing (@DrLizMBSHealing)

Videos

Dr. Liz "How I Self-Published on Amazon and Became a #1 Multi-International Best-Selling Author":
https://youtu.be/yGFm6oiUdFg

Audiobook
trailer: https://videos.files.wordpress.com/s4QN5UbB/life-launch-trailer_hd.mp4

Donate

The BJD Rainbow of Hope Foundation for Suicide Prevention and Mental Health:
https://www.paypal.com/donate/?hosted_button_id=2DDLVM9 EEAY74

QR Code

Table of Contents

Introduction
Progress Not Perfection

For readers of all ages who have struggled or are struggling with the dilemma of how to live life on life's terms. The collection of poems which follows was written by the author, who has travelled down the treacherous road of depression, co-dependence, terrifying insecurity and even addiction. The writings describe the author's journey through her tumultuous teens, which includes a number of poems dealing with the death of her brother, prose about other family members, and many poems and writings about the elation and devastation of love and relationships

(These were the some of the first words I wrote in my tweens, around 1975)

People

(People in my life let me down often…)

People are so human I can't stand it!

So ignorant to recognize change

So ignorant to change themselves.

It's so sad….

Life goes on…

Yet no one goes out of their way to do something

nice

<u>*"What the world needs now, is love, sweet love..."*</u>

<u>*~The Carpenters*</u>

(Written in the late 70's, mid-teens)

These words have no doubt been quoted a thousand times, let this be one thousand one. I contend that this is still true – but perhaps the real problem is that we need to know <u>how</u> to love. How often is it that we have no difficulty telling someone <u>what</u> they need, but are completely oblivious to the fact that they may not know <u>how</u> to achieve or acquire that necessary thing.

<u>I Love You, You are my Favorite Thing</u>

I love you, you are my favorite thing.

Like flowers blooming in the spring.

Like breezes blowing through my hair.

Like perfection needing no repair.

I love you, you are my favorite thing.

<u>Roses</u>

Roses, roses in the air!

The sweet smell of flowers everywhere.

The rustling leaves, the bare trees,

All I see is Mystery.

<u>Moonshine</u>

The moon is shining bright tonight.

I wish you were here to hold me tight.

It's nice to be with you, to hold you near,

To look in your eyes and escape all fear.

Like the moon, you are quiet but strong, with you

I feel like I belong.

Together I know we can't go wrong.

<u>Uncertainty of Life</u>

(Written on March 2nd, 1976, just a couple of weeks before I turned 13 y.o. and 6 days before my brother died from the broken neck he suffered in a Feb. 7th , 1976 car accident – hit by a drunk driver who was speeding.)

How much more can I take?

How much longer can I last?

Will it ever stop?

Will the nagging doubt ever stop?

When will it happen?

Will it ever happen?

Will it ever stop?

<u>Yet...</u>

(Written on March 3rd, 1976, again notice the timing to me entering my teens, puberty and to my brother's death. He was in the hospital in a semi-comatose state from the accident on 2/7/76 until he passed on 3/8/76.)

The sun is setting, yet there still is light

The trees are dying, yet there is still growth

The grass is wet, yet it keeps on growing

The moon is gone, yet it keeps on shining

A man is gone, yet he tries to fight.

<u>13 y.o. Self-Talk about Life & Death</u>

(Written on April 7, 1976, 13 y.o.)

Life gives you many tragedies and hard times

If you fall while doing something,

pick yourself up and go on with life.

If one of your loved ones must go.

You must continue with your life and

take it all in stride – it will always be hard,

but you have to live with it.

If you ever need to consult someone about this –

the Lord is always there.

<u>What is Love?</u>

Love is so hard. I wish it was easier. Sometimes
it's nice, sometimes it's not. I love but, why is it
so mixed up… Or am I?

God is Love

(Written 3/4/76, 12 y.o, 4 days before my brother died)

You are wise 'cause you can see.

All the things that I can be.

You can see me inside out,

You are love without a doubt.

Who Am I?

She sits in her room all by herself,

thinking about the day,

About how she could lie to herself saying,

"I am just that way."

She is not that way at all and she will never be.

'Cause no one can change the way she is,

not her or even me.

<u>*Life*</u>

She peeks out behind a marshmallow cloud –

but no one notices in the crowd.

"How is it done?" I asked to me.

No one knows, not even she.

Deep, deep down,

Under the glittering surface

There I stared, but for what purpose?

Then when I saw it happen again,

Life passed me by; but I know not when.

<u>*Not Ready for Spring*</u>

(Written in the Spring of 1976, after my brother passed away.)

The smell of spring is in the air,

Pretty flowers everywhere.

One kind soul who cannot be there,

We will cherish him everywhere.

1st *Teenage Love*

(Written in 12/4/78 @ 15 y.o.)

I love you Joe,

I love you so,

I hope our love will ever grow.

The winter's come,

The cold is here,

I need you, love, so near so near.

Hear me then and help me to

figure out what I should do.

<u>*Dear Joe*</u>

ME LUVS you

ME LUVS you

Do you Luvs ME TOO?

You Luvs ME

You Luvs ME

Let's GET AWAY

Do what we do

Feelings

(Written 12/28, late 70's)

I've got to be strong right now, but it's rough.

My eyes want to cry, but my mind says, "Be

tough!"

I need someone bad. I need someone now.

Oh, I wish he was here to show me how to laugh

and talk and love with life- to get away from all

this strife!

For Ever More

The silent waters trickling by,

The deep blueness of the sky,

These and others I hold dear,

When it is you I long to be near

Gently twinkling are your eyes,

And your honesty shows you tell no lies.

Some say, "You'll lose him I know for sure."

But I know we're together for evermore.

Like spires rising in the sky

My thoughts of you are ever high.

I think of you, day in, day out.

And when I can't see you,

I lie and pout.

Many times you go astray

And do not listen to what I say

But I can't stay angry at you for long –

So I forgive you and sing a song!

Authenticity

(Written 12/26/78, 15 y.o.)

The sun is bright,

I feel alright

with you sitting here beside me.

Your face, your eyes,

your hair, no lies.

It's nice being with you.

Trish, Us

(Written around 1978 about my best friend)

Silent, growing,

attached yet   separate

We cling to each other for advice, patience, fun.

Separate   we   are   helpless,

Together we are strong.

<u>Mr. Frisch</u>

**(Written around 1978 for my freshman HS English teacher.
I was still so sad from losing my brother and still so
confused about life and its meaning – looking for answers.
He was one of the few male teachers who never took
advantage of me, never was inappropriate, and he did
whatever he could to help me navigate this difficult time in
my life.)**

He's big and neat and very sweet

and makes me smile all over.

He helps me learn, that at every turn,

there's more and more to uncover.

His big blue eyes say, "Oh,

there's such a long, long way to go."

"I know there is, but

the problems are here,

And it's hard to let go

of someone so dear."

I feel lost and alone,

like a big empty home,

with no one to keep it warm.

I need a strong arm, one that won't

harm, to keep me safe from fear.

Oh, will you be my big brother

and help me discover

the things I need to know?

The things that don't always show.

Teach me and tell me the earth,

the sky, the ear, the eye,

the falling of rain and snow.

Grandmom

(Written around 1978, 16 y.o.)

Grandmoms are the sweetest things,
The fondest memories to my mind
they bring.
The summer shore, an evening walk
The kind, caring way they talk.

Grandmoms never miss a day,
Your graduation, vacation…
A greeting is always on its way.

Very seldom do you hear an unkind word,
However, in their silence, their concern is
often heard. Grandmom, this poem is for
your eighty years,
Of caring, sharing, and shedding tears.

For smiling, grandmom and just being
you…
This party is the very least we could do! *

~This letter was written with this poem~
This poem says in a nutshell all the things I
remember about you, Gram. But, the fondest

memories I have are of our summers down the shore.

I remember taking walks out to the big white bench at the end of the driveway and sitting on it and talking with you. In the morning, I loved to watch the bird bath in the middle of the only patch of grass in the yard. And you taught me not to get too close to the birds or the birds would fly away. You used to watch from your kitchen window while you did the breakfast dishes, but I was too little to look out.

I used to hope that you hadn't cut the sweet-smelling roses yet, so I could help you with it. But even if you had, I liked to go back there and smell them anyway.

I think my favorite smell of all was the attic. I looked forward to going up there and exploring. It was like a secret room in the house. I remember the night my sister and I slept up there. You and Grandpop, Mom and Dad were downstairs watching the Olympics and we could hear everything that you said. But we were in a different world than you were. We were like two little mice in our own home. I remember feeling warm and safe and content.

Gram, these are the kind of feelings memories of you bring to mind. The kinds of memories and feelings which have become a part of me and won't be forgotten. The greatest joy is not only in reminiscing, but in sharing them with others that you love and love you back.

Happy birthday Gram, and may the Lord bless you with many more.

I love you,
Liz

The Key of E

(Written around 1978, 16 y.o.)

He says the Key of E's the most beautiful

He says it's the best one to play

So I'll sing this one for him in E

If he'll listen to his heart today

When our eyes first met

We both felt struck

By something we did not know.

Was it love so soon?

Or just a trick of the moon?

Sing it in E and we'll know

I'll sing "I love you" in E

If it makes you truly happy

I'll sing "I miss you" in E

If you'll say you miss me too

For she has your ring and only part of your love

But I'm the one you're dreamin' of

I'm the one you're dreamin' of

I'm the one for you

He sang, "You swept me off my feet"

I said "you did me too"

Won't you hear me sing in the key of E

"Don't leave me now, I'm blue"

"Don't leave me now, I'm true"

<u>Prayer</u>

Dear Lord,

The wonders of thy majestic works never cease to

amaze me. The intricate designs of the grass, the

trees, the skies;

The forest, field and stream;

And the flower – thy lovely flower of beauty

abundant,

Unfolding its petals with the first golden rays of

dawn,

Stretching its roots deep into the soft earth,

seeking food and strength and nourishment from

you.

For you are everywhere.

Your love is in every breath that I breathe, every

step that I take, every hand that I hold.

You never cease to amaze me Lord,

I truly love thy ways.   Amen.

The Faith of my Parents

We are here to carry on what was begun by one.

To live according to his love and faith through his
son,

To love spontaneously, to give unselfishly to
those who need your help,

To lend an ear and wait to hear what he's got to
say,

'Cos it might be you who's got the blues and
needs someone someday.

<u>Nature's Solace</u>

When I look at the majestic trees,

and feel the rhythm of the brisk blowing breeze,

My thoughts float up and out of sight

soar to the moon and stars of night.

There I feel so important and safe

and no one can kick me out of place.

But when I'm away from the beautiful trees,

and nature's brisk blowing motherly breeze.

I no longer can say what I feel or do as I please.

<u>Dreams for a Lifetime</u>

(This was about a forbidden love I had with someone much older. I hoped it would last forever, but somehow knew it wouldn't, therefore, I intuitively titled the poem "Dreams for a Lifetime" because I knew that would be all I have left when it was over.)

Your hug is like the warm rays of the sun,

which envelope me in its stillness.

Your kiss is as soft and sweet as the petals of a

rose and its luscious fragrance.

My love, when we walk hand in hand in peaceful

contentment through the waters of life,

The blows are but ripples on the sweet pink

water, for you are there to calm them.

And the happy times are more enjoyable

when you are there to share them.

I love you deeper than the blueness of the sky at

night, And my love for you is stronger than the

pull of gravity which keeps my feet on the ground

For if there was no gravity, I would certainly soar
to the stars and the moon,
And there forever stay, until your face was no
longer there to hold me up.
Love, Liz

<u>*You are My World*</u>

You're my one and only love.

You make me smile and look above

all the obstacles in our way

'cause you know our love won't go away.

You make me strong when I am weak,

You calm me down when I'm at my peak.

You love me so and I love you-

Our love transcends the ocean blue.

The kind and gentle words you say

take all my cares and worries away.

And each time you touch me it's something new.

For you learn me and I learn you.

Now you are a part of me and I a part of you

And nothing can come between us

Because we are together now and forever

Our love, our life means thus.

**(You guessed it, this was about the same forbidden love as
"Dreams for a Lifetime")**

<u>Greetings</u>

(I entertained the idea of writing greeting card content and selling it to American Greetings or Hallmark)

Just a little note sent your way,

to tell you how I feel and to say

That you're thought about and loved each day,

And friends I hope we will forever stay.

<u>Ode to a Forbidden Love</u>

(Written on or about 08/24/1979, my 16th year)

He's quiet and calm and gentle too,

He's what I need,

I NEED YOU!

~Love, Liz

<u>I love You</u>

I Love You, Sean,

I Love You so,

And I know together we will always grow.

Your tenderness and strength

will go to great lengths

to always keep me near.

But you need not fear

'Cos I'll be here

Ready to disappear…

XXOO ★

Fred

(Written on or about 08/29/1979. This was another infatuation with an older man – about 16 yrs. my senior – I was 17 and he was in his early 30's. I'm so glad I saved this because it is proof of how naïve I was! (i.e. not understanding why he was so cautious with me…geez!) Well, my Higher Power was looking out for me, because Fred was very kind to me!)

Dear Fred,

Hi Love! How've you been? I hope fine – I'm pretty well, There's lots of things I would like to talk to you about. Mainly has to do with that question I asked you when we were joggin' – "Why are you so cautious with me?" If you want to talk about it, I'm ready when you are!

There's a lot more I could say but I'll save it for when we talk.

Thanks for listenin'.

I love you!   Love always, Liz.

Unbridled NOW

(Written on 9/21/79, 16 y.o. I was expressing trying to not go so fast in a relationship and ruin it, my reference to "too late!". I was always living in tomorrow (because my "today" was so unpleasant), so here I share my struggle with staying focused on the here and now.)

As the pillowy clouds drift overhead,

I know I've got to obey red.

Just slow down and wait

before I open the next gate.

See what's now

and work with it somehow

Or else it'll be too late!

NOW…

<u>A Song For Someone</u>

(Written on 12/2/79, 16 y.o.)

Fresh as sunshine, sweet as rain,

I know that I won't be the same without you.

<u>Open Arms</u>

My love extends with outstretched arms.

As my arms open up, so does my heart.

When my arms begin to fold, so does my heart.

When my heart closes, I die.

<u>*Your Eyes*</u>

(Written in 3/17/82, 19 y.o.)

Through the window of your mind,

In the playland of love,

Infinitely long and eternally wide.

A world full of unicorns, rainbows and

wishes...

Everything mythical and magical.

A place where memories and dreams

reside.

Memories as enjoyable as carnation

in bloom,

Dreams as permanent as the beauty

of a dew-covered rose

This is where I want to dwell with

you.

In a world of happiness and love

<u>*My Sweet Prince*</u>

The sweet music I hear reminds me of our first

kiss.

How long ago was that; yet only seems like

yesterday

when you took me in your arms and held me

tightly,

loving away all my worries.

And the days I said, "Good-bye. I can't see you

anymore."

But soon returned once again to you because I

couldn't stay away.

My Prince, you are the song in my heart,

never to be sung for anyone else.

Simply Codependent

How can I be me,

without making it difficult for you to be you?

I love you

My Sister

I felt a tremendous closeness while

near her tonight.

I felt like hugging her and holding

her tight,

Like crying away all the sadness

that we had brought each other.

I feel like a vulnerable, innocent

child.

People Revisited

People, people, people.
People are so, so, so interesting.

I really love people,
Especially this type.

Talk, talk, talk
Getting to know people is important.

I love people.

I wish I could show them
how much I love them.

<u>*The Invitation*</u>

(Written sometime in between 1983-'88)

With the golden rays of the sun's

outstretched arms,

I too beckon to you:
Come, fly with me.

Come, on the never-ending journey

to the center of the Earth

to the core of the soul

to the depths of the seas.

Once you're there, you cannot leave.

Once you grasp, you cannot let go.

It's an infinite mercy-go-round.

It's Laughter
It's Life
It's Love.

One Saturday in March

(Written around March 1988, 25 y.o.)

And so we sit…

Gently caressing our bodies in the warmth of the

fire.

The window panes sometimes shivering

under the force of wind – blown rain drops.

The ocean beyond,

Carrying determined fisherman towards

their evening meals

And reveling joyously in the return of

moisture to its home.

This day we sit, my love and I,

and contemplate-

What has been…
What is now…
What may be…

<u>Lessons from my Grandmother</u>

We are here to carry on what was begun by one.

To live according to His love and faith through

His son;

To love spontaneously, to give unselfishly to

those who need your help,

To lend an ear and wait to hear what they've got

to say,

'Cos it might be you who's got the blues and

needs someone someday.

~LB

Until We Die

(Written around 1983, 20 y.o.)

When you put your arms around me

and look deep into my eyes,

For that moment I'm a queen – You're around me

And you're my King – I'm satisfied

For that instance, nothing else exists

Except for you and I

And together we shall go, as God insists,

Caring for one another until we die.

My love for you is boundless,

It's a never-ending sea.

And remember, there's never anyone around

us

Whenever you put your arms around me

<u>Heart to D i s t a n t Heart</u>

(Written Fall of 2011, 48 y.o.)

My Heart cries out for You
In the darkness
When my mind is quiet
from its toil
of distracting My Heart from Its Pain.

There's No Reply - You're Not There

Just

empty   s p a c e

and tears f
a
l l
like Rain...   i
n
g

Across the miles
My Heart searches for Yours
At one time joined?
Now it's certain
To Mine, Yours never was...

<u>*Thank You For Reading!!!*</u>

If you would be so kind as to leave a review* of my book on Amazon, I would greatly appreciate your feedback!

***Go to your "Orders" or "Digital Orders" page and click on "Write a product review"**

Coming soon — *Book Two: LIFE LAUNCH! A New Dawn of Healing and Recovery*

Visit my Website for FREEBIES, videos, my blog, to connect, follow and subscribe to my social media channels:
<u>http://www.drlizlifelaunch.com</u>

Healing Webinar: <u>www.mbshealingwebinars.com</u>

Acknowledgements

Much thanks goes out to M. Scott Peck, author of the Road Less Travelled, for teaching me what love is and how to love; to Narcotics Anonymous, Alcoholics Anonymous and my sponsors over the years for teaching me how to use the 12-step programs which provide daily insight (for those who seek it) into accepting life on life's terms and to my Higher Power for always being there for strength, guidance, love and freedom from fear.

I am deeply indebted to my sister-friend, Stacey Ann Sadouly for transcribing all of these works off of old, faded papers, over 40 years old, and getting them into the computer! I also thank her very much for suggesting titles for a good number of these poems. I think she chose splendidly!